The Daily

Psalms

Kristi Burchfiel

ISBN-13: 978-1500284800
ISBN-10: 1500284807

Cover design by Jonna Feavel
Images used with permission
ID 23521024 © **Clearviewstock** | Dreamstime.com
ID 22253306 © **Cynoclub** | Dreamstime.com
Swirl ©Andrea Haase|Dreamstime.com

Unless otherwise identified, all scripture quotations in this publication are taken from *New American Standard Bible*®, Copyright © 1960, 1962, 1963, 1968, 1971, 1972, 1973, 1975, 1977, 1995 by The Lockman Foundation.

Introduction

What is The Daily Devotional Series?

The Daily Devotional Series was born from my own personal devotions. As part of my daily time with God, I wanted to be able to read and study a whole book of the Bible at a time. However, I also wanted to be able to focus on one specific thought or idea that I could hold on to for the whole day.

Ultimately, I decided to take one book of the Bible, read through one chapter a day, and then focus on a truth from one verse in that chapter. This allows me to balance the consistency of going through a whole book at a time with the specific focus I need for that particular day.

These devotions are not designed to be an in-depth study of a particular verse, chapter, or book. They are intentionally designed to be brief. Because of this, readers won't get bogged down in lots of theology. Instead, I encourage the reader to take the time to really focus on application in his or her personal life. The Bible is living and active and applicable in our daily lives.

How do I use The Daily Devotional Series?

If you have the time, I encourage you to take the time to read through the entire chapter for each day so you can get the full story and background information. However, realize that is not necessary to be able to follow and learn from the devotionals. Each devotional focuses on one verse, the truth in that verse, and a response to pray back to God.

May you be blessed as you study God's word and apply it to your life daily.

About Psalms

For centuries, people have used songs as a way to share their feelings and emotions. Ideas that were difficult to express in words alone could be brought to life and given deeper meaning when put to music.

The book of Psalms is, in essence, the hymnbook of the Bible. The songs here are written by multiple authors over a span of almost 1000 years. These were later compiled into five "books" which make up Psalms. The songs address historical events, personal struggles, emotional triumphs, betrayals, and so many more issues. Through them all, God's glory is evident and praised. These songs give examples from people who are feeling some of life's rawest and deepest emotions, and they still continue to trust in God.

Psalm a wonderful book to read and meditate on. These verses offer encouragement, hope, and peace. Several of the songs are prophetic in nature and directly refer to the coming redeemer, Jesus Christ. Many of the words from the Psalms are quoted throughout the New Testament by several authors, including Jesus Christ himself. For example, Psalm 22 is an almost direct representation of the crucifixion of Jesus Christ, with Jesus quoting directly from the psalm while hanging on the cross.

Since these chapters are segmented into 5 books, each book has a general theme and idea that can be found through those chapters. Book 1 contains chapters 1 through 41. These psalms are primarily written by King David. Prominent through these first psalms is the idea of mankind being blessed, fallen, and then ultimately redeemed by God. Through these songs we see the special relationship that God has with man and how He will provide forgiveness and restoration to the person who will seek after God.

Book 2 includes chapters 42 through 72. Most of these psalms are written by King David, whose life is detailed in 1 Samuel 16 through 1 Kings 2. These particular psalms typically focus on the ruin and then restoration through God. God is the solution to all the concerns that we have, and we can trust Him and bring our concerns to Him.

Book 3 contains chapters 73 through 89. The majority of these psalms are attributed to the authorship of Asaph. Asaph is mentioned in 1 Chronicles 15:19 as one of the singers in the temple during the time of David. These are psalms of praise and reverence and worship, similar to songs we might expect to hear in a house of worship today.

Book 4 is made up of chapters 90 through 106. Most of these psalms are anonymously written. These psalms typically address the idea that we are part of God's kingdom and we can trust that God's kingdom will rule over all others. We can rest in His rule and His reign over all.

Book 5 includes chapters 107 through 150. Many of these psalms were written by King David and most are hymns of praise that were used in the people's corporate worship services. In these psalms you will see a definite focus on the praise and worship of a Holy God. He is great and amazing and the psalmists describe God's characteristics so that we give Him all praise.

While each and every chapter has a story behind it which is worthy of study, I want point out two specific areas before we dive into the devotions. First, Psalm

119 has the distinction of being the longest chapter in the Bible. This chapter has 176 verses and is split into sections of eight verses. In the original Hebrew, each section corresponds to a letter of the Hebrew alphabet, so the first eight verses all begin with the letter "aleph," the next eight verses all begin with the letter "beth," and so on through all 22 letters of the Hebrew alphabet. This chapter is also considered a love chapter to the Word of God. Over and over throughout the chapter, God's word is praised and lifted up.

Second, chapters 120 – 134 had a special purpose for the people of Israel. These are called the "Songs of Ascents" or "Pilgrim Psalms." These psalms were sung by those who were journeying to the temple for the annual feasts. As you read through these psalms you can really get a picture of how the people were preparing their hearts for worship while they journeyed. These psalms make an excellent group to study in preparation for worship.

Regardless of what issue you are facing, what circumstance you find yourself in, or what emotion you are experiencing, chances are very good that there is a psalm which will address it. Allow yourself to feel the emotions of the various authors and learn from their faith as they rejoice in the Creator of all during both the highs and lows of life.

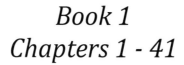

Book 1
Chapters 1 - 41

Chapter 1

Psalm 1:1—How blessed is the man who does not walk in the counsel of the wicked, nor stand in the path of sinners, nor sit in the seat of scoffers!

TRUTH:
Where do we find our counsel? Who do we look to for advice and guidance? We are to plant ourselves firmly in Christ and receive our guidance only from Him and others who follow Him. We need to be constantly aware of who we are around and how they influence us. Do they influence us to me more like Christ?

RESPONSE:
Lord, I want to walk only in Your counsel, stand in Your path, and sit by Your throne. I will seek others who will encourage me in following You.

Chapter 2

Psalm 2:11—Worship the Lord with reverence and rejoice with trembling.

TRUTH:
The Lord is worthy of all our worship and praise. He is amazing, and His power and might are worthy of our respect. Do we not only praise the Lord, but praise Him in a way that is honoring and respectful of the power He possesses?

RESPONSE:
Father, You are so many things, including powerful and just. I praise You for Your righteousness and holiness!

Chapter 3

Psalm 3:2-3—Many are saying of my soul, "There is no deliverance for him in God." Selah. But You, O Lord, are a shield about me, My glory, and the One who lifts my head.

TRUTH:
People and going to try and tell us that God won't be there for us or that He will fail and disappoint us. However, the Lord is the One who shields us, gives us glory, and lifts up our head. Will we listen to others or follow the truth of who God is?

RESPONSE:
Lord, many people have tried to pull me away from trusting You. Keep me steadfast. Help me to live in the truth of who You are and what You do for me.

Chapter 4

Psalm 4:8—In peace I will lie down and sleep, for You alone, O Lord, make me to dwell in safety.

TRUTH:
So many things promise but then fail to provide. Our security and protection is found only in Christ. Only by trusting Him completely can we find peace. Are we lacking peace in any area of our life? Then we need to place our trust in God for that area and rest in His peace.

RESPONSE:
Lord, You know every area of my life. I place them all in Your hand and dwell in Your peace and safety.

Chapter 5

Psalm 5:3—In the morning, O Lord, You will hear my voice; in the morning I will order my prayer to You and eagerly watch.

TRUTH:
Can the Lord expect to hear our voice every morning? Or do we just come to Him when we have a problem? When we do pray to Him, are we eagerly watching for His response? Or do we press ahead without Him and try to answer our own prayers? God wants to be in a relationship with us, not just a recipient of our information. We must trust Him and come to Him consistently and expectantly.

RESPONSE:
Lord, I love to bring my prayers to You. Help me to wait and watch for You to answer, not try to answer my own prayers.

Chapter 6

Psalm 6:4—Return, O Lord, rescue my soul; save me because of Your lovingkindness.

TRUTH:
The Lord is the rescuer. He is able to save us, not only from eternal death, but also from the day-to-day difficulties we encounter. Do we call to Him in the midst of all our trials?

RESPONSE:
Lord, You are loving and You delight in rescuing those of us who ask. Lord, save me from the evil one because of Your lovingkindness.

Chapter 7

Psalm 7:1—O Lord my God, in You I have taken refuge; save me from all those who pursue me, and deliver me.

TRUTH:
When we go through difficulties, do we not just pray to God for help, but actually realign ourselves so that we are taking refuge in the Lord? He is our only refuge and only in Him can we find salvation and deliverance.

RESPONSE:
God, I pray that You will help me to not only ask for Your deliverance, but to actually move so that I take refuge in You.

Chapter 8

Psalm 8:8—Yet You have made him a little lower than God, and You crown him with glory and majesty!

TRUTH:
As humans, we must remember two things. First, we are created by God, we are not gods ourselves. We must never allow God's position in our life to be altered. Second, as His creation, we have a glory and a majesty that God gives that is reflective of Yours. We are like no other creation of His; we are crowned with His glory and majesty!

RESPONSE:
Lord, help me to go through today knowing that You are over all, and You have chosen to crown me with glory and honor so that I reflect Yours. Help me live my life pointing people to the One who gives the glory and honor.

Chapter 9

Psalm 9:10—And those who know Your name will put their trust in You, for You, O Lord, have not forsaken those who seek You.

TRUTH:
God promises that if we are seeking after Him, He will not forsake us. He is worthy of our trust. Do we need a reminder of God's faithfulness today? Seek after Him; He will be there every time just as He promises.

RESPONSE:
Lord, You are faithful and trustworthy. I place my trust in You. I lean on Your promise and will share it with others today.

Chapter 10

Psalm 10:4—The wicked in the haughtiness of his countenance, does not seek Him. All his thoughts are, "There is no God."

TRUTH:
Often we will talk like we believe and trust God, yet live our lives as if there is no God. Do we truly trust God in every area of our life and do our actions display that trust?

RESPONSE:
Lord, I want my every action to speak of You and all You can do. Forgive me when I try to do things on my own and teach me how to trust You more.

Chapter 11

Psalm 11:7—For the Lord is righteous, He loves righteousness; the upright will behold His face.

TRUTH:
God is holy and righteous. Yet God promises us that if we are upright and seeking Him, we will behold His face. Do we see God's face in everything we are going through?

RESPONSE:
Lord, Your face is what I seek. As You are righteous, Lord help me live righteous in Your sight.

Chapter 12

Psalm 12:5—"Because of the devastation of the afflicted, because of the groaning of the needy, now I will arise," says the Lord; "I will set him in the safety for which he longs."

TRUTH:
The Lord hears us and will come protect and defend us. Do we cry out to Him in our times of need? He promises to set us in safety. Our safety is only found in Him.

RESPONSE:
Lord, only in Your protection am I truly safe. I pray that I will come to You first for every need I have. You hear my groaning and answer.

Chapter 13

Psalm 13:5—But I have trusted in Your lovingkindness; my heart shall rejoice in Your salvation.

TRUTH:
David was going through difficult times. He was down and despairing and yet, even in these dark times, he trusted and rejoiced in the Lord. When we go through hard times do we still trust and cling to the Lord?

RESPONSE:
Father, thank You for being worthy of my trust. Even in the dark times, I will rejoice in You.

Chapter 14

Psalm 14:1—The fool has said in his heart, "There is no God." They are corrupt, they have committed abominable deeds; there is no one who does good.

TRUTH:
If we are busy trying to be good on our own, then we are being foolish. No one is good outside of Jesus. Only a fool tries to live without God. Are we surrendering to God and allowing Him to direct us? Or, are we trying on our own and looking foolish to God?

RESPONSE:
Lord, I need You in every area of my life. Help me to not be foolish and try to do things on my own. Direct my every path today.

Chapter 15

Psalm 15:1—O Lord, who may abide in Your tent? Who may dwell on Your holy hill?

TRUTH:
What does God require of us? The rest of this psalm answers this question by describing the actions of perfection that God requires. We cannot get to God on our own, but we can allow Jesus in our life to live that perfect life for us. Only Jesus is the answer to the question above. Is He living in and through us?

RESPONSE:
Lord, thank You for providing a substitute who lived the life You require for us so that through Him, we may abide in Your tent and dwell with You!

Chapter 16

Psalm 16:11—You will make known to me the path of life; in Your presence is fullness of joy; in Your right hand there are pleasures forever.

TRUTH:
In God we find life, joy, and pleasure. He holds these gifts in His hand and is just waiting for us to come to Him. Will we seek out God for our joy or do we try unsuccessfully to get it on our own?

RESPONSE:
Lord, only through You is there true life, joy, and pleasure. Help me to seek these only through You.

Chapter 17

Psalm 17:1—Hear a just cause, O Lord, give heed to my cry; give ear to my prayer, which is not from deceitful lips.

TRUTH:
When we come to God in prayer, are we honest with Him? Or do we just pray about trivial things in our life and not the true issues we are facing? For me, it can be easy to just gloss over prayer and to not always take the time to share my deepest concerns with Him. Do we pray with passion for the things we want to see Him take control of in our lives?

RESPONSE:
Lord, I come to You truthfully admitting where I am. You see me anyway, and I need You in every area of my life!

Chapter 18

Psalm 18:17—He delivered me from my strong enemy, and from those who hated me, for they were too mighty for me.

TRUTH:
If we trust in the Lord and wait on Him, He will deliver us from our enemies. He is the refuge from our strong enemy. He shields us from their mighty attacks. Are we taking refuge in God or still trying to fight on our own?

RESPONSE:
Lord, I praise You for being a place of refuge and safety for me. The enemy is strong; help me to turn to You.

Chapter 19

Psalm 19:1—The heavens are telling the glory of God; and their expanse is declaring the work of His hands.

TRUTH:
All around us, God's presence is evident in the beauty of His creation. Do we praise Him for the wonders He has created? Do we thank Him for allowing us to share in His amazing and beautiful creations?

RESPONSE:
Lord, Your creation displays Your glory, wonder, power, and creativity. Your works are glorious and today I will praise You.

Chapter 20

Psalm 20:1—May the Lord answer you in the day of trouble! May the name of the God of Jacob set you securely on high!

TRUTH:
The Lord is there for us when we are going through difficulties. He is our security and He keeps us directly in His will. There will be days of trouble, but we can know that God is our security in all of our circumstances.

RESPONSE:
Lord, I praise You for Your love, protection, and security in all things. You are amazing and while there will be days of trouble, You will be there with me.

Chapter 21

Psalm 21:7—For the king trusts in the Lord, and through the lovingkindness of the Most High he will not be shaken.

TRUTH:
King David wrote this psalm. He knew that even though he was the king, he could not take care of things on his own. Instead, he trusted in the Lord. He was not shaken because He had God's lovingkindness. Like David, we can stand firm and trust God. His lovingkindness will hold us firm even when everything around us is shaking.

RESPONSE:
Lord, thank You for holding me steady with Your lovingkindness I know that nothing I encounter today will be able to shake me.

Chapter 22

Psalm 22:8—Commit yourself to the Lord; let Him deliver him, let Him rescue him, because He delights in him.

TRUTH:
The Lord does delight in us. He will rescue us. We are to commit ourselves to Him. Are we expecting the rewards without the commitment? The Lord seeks both commitment to Him and our permission for Him to be allowed to act in and through us. Will we let Him?

RESPONSE:
Lord, I commit myself to You. I will let You deliver and rescue me and not try to do these things on my own.

Chapter 23

Psalm 23:1—The Lord is my shepherd, I shall not want.

TRUTH:
Do we find ourselves wanting for anything? The Lord is our shepherd, our protector, our provider, and our guide. Through Him all our needs are provided for. Are we following our shepherd in every area of our life?

RESPONSE:
Lord, You are my shepherd. I will follow where You lead me and through You, I will want for nothing.

Chapter 24

Psalm 24:8—Who is this King of glory? The Lord strong and mighty, the Lord mighty in battle.

TRUTH:
Who is it that we serve and put our faith and trust in? The Lord is strong and mighty and worthy of our praise. Do we take the time to get to know the King of glory? He desires a relationship with us.

RESPONSE:
Father, help me to know You better today and to share who you are with others. You are the Lord, strong and mighty!

Chapter 25

Psalm 25:5—Lead me in Your truth and teach me, for You are the God of my salvation; for You I wait all the day.

TRUTH:

This is a beautiful prayer asking God to lead and reveal Himself for who He is. Are we willing to be led and taught? Are we willing to wait on Him? Are we willing to pray this prayer to Him today?

RESPONSE:

Lord, I need this in my life for You are my salvation. Please lead me in Your truth and teach me. I will wait for You all day!

Chapter 26

Psalm 26:2—Examine me, O Lord, and try me; test my mind and my heart.

TRUTH:
Are we willing to submit to an examination from the Lord? What will He find when he looks? The Lord is looking for obedience and a willing heart. He wants to fill each of us with Himself. We must be willing to let go of the ordinary things in our life in order for that to happen. Are we willing to allow Christ to examine and fill every part of our life with Himself?

RESPONSE:
Lord, look through my life, my mind, and my heart. Remove anything that doesn't meet Your standards and replace it with Yourself.

Chapter 27

Psalm 27:14—Wait for the Lord; be strong and let your heart take courage; yes, wait for the Lord.

TRUTH:
We don't often think of courage and strength being the same as patience. The Lord indicates that waiting on Him takes strength and courage. Will we be strong and wait on the Lord? Will we show our courage by displaying our patience?

RESPONSE:
Lord, I will wait on You. Help me to be strong and courageous by waiting on You today.

Chapter 28

Psalm 28:9—Save Your people and bless Your inheritance; be their shepherd also, and carry them forever.

TRUTH:
Salvation, blessing, guidance, and support. These four areas show how the Lord touches our lives if we will choose to let Him. He wants to provide for us as we are His people and His inheritance. His touch in our lives lasts forever.

RESPONSE:
Father, thank You for Your salvation and Your blessings. I praise You for guiding me and supporting me throughout every day.

Chapter 29

Psalm 29:2—Ascribe to the Lord the glory due to His name; worship the Lord in holy array.

TRUTH:
The Lord is worthy of glory. Do we give Him the glory and praise that He is due? His name is above every other name. Do we live our daily lives reflecting that glory to others?

RESPONSE:
Lord, You are worthy of all glory and all power. All praise is due You. Help me to reflect Your glory to everyone I am around today.

Chapter 30

Psalm 30:11—You have turned for me my mourning into dancing; You have loosed my sackcloth and girded me with gladness.

TRUTH:
As we go through this life, we will experience sadness and difficulties. The Lord wants us to rest in Him. He is the only one who can take our hard times and turn them into dancing and gladness. Do we let Him have our troubles or do we just hold on to them ourselves?

RESPONSE:
Father, Your ability to make something beautiful out of the ugly in my life is amazing. Take all that is ugly and do with it as you see fit. Thank You for transforming my life.

Chapter 31

Psalm 31:3—For You are my rock and my fortress; for Your name's sake You will lead me and guide me.

TRUTH:
Because we trust in the Lord, other people around us know it and are watching how we respond to various situations. When we go through difficulties, we can trust God to care for us and strengthen us, not just for our own benefit, but also as a witness to the others who know we trust in God as well.

RESPONSE:
Lord, You show Yourself trustworthy and faithful in every circumstance. Thank You for Your care and guidance. Help me to be a witness to Your faithfulness no matter what situation I go through today.

Chapter 32

Psalm 32:5—I acknowledged my sin to You, and my iniquity I did not hide; I said, "I will confess my transgressions to the Lord," and You forgave the guilt of my sin.

TRUTH:
God knows all things, including our sins. But He wants us to confess them to Him to confirm that we know what we have done wrong. Do we acknowledge and confess our sin? God is waiting to forgive the sin itself as well as the guilt caused by the sin.

RESPONSE:
Lord, I bring my shortcomings to You. I have failed You in so many ways. Please forgive me and restore me today.

Chapter 33

Psalm 33:1—Sing for joy in the Lord, O you righteous ones; praise is becoming to the upright.

TRUTH:
We are never more beautiful to God than when we are praising Him. When we tell of God's glory and give Him praise, regardless of our personal circumstances, God is pleased and it adds to our beauty. The Lord takes great joy and delight in our words and deeds of praise.

RESPONSE:
Lord, I praise You, I am thankful for You, and I lift You up. I will sing for joy to You in every circumstance.

Chapter 34

Psalm 34:18—The Lord is near to the brokenhearted and saves those who are crushed in spirit.

TRUTH:
Those who are hurting can find their comfort in the Lord. He promises to be close and to save those who are broken in heart and crushed in spirit. Do we sense Him in the midst of our dark times? Are we even looking for Him in the midst of the darkness of circumstances? Do we allow Him to comfort us?

RESPONSE:
Lord, You walk through my hard times with me. Hold me and guide me. Be near and save me.

Chapter 35

Psalm 35:20—For they do not speak peace, but they devise deceitful words against those who are quiet in the land.

TRUTH:
Even if we are following Jesus in every way, there will be people who say wrong things and lie about us. How do we respond when we are wrongfully accused? Instead of complaining to anyone and everyone, we should bring our concerns to God. He is our defender and protector. He will lead us in how to respond to those people.

RESPONSE:
Lord, when others speak wrong against me, I pray You will defend me. I will wait on You to lead my every step.

Chapter 36

Psalm 36:7—How precious is Your lovingkindness, O God! And the children of men take refuge in the shadow of Your wings.

TRUTH:
We need the Lord's lovingkindness to make it through our day. We can take refuge from the storms of life in God who protects us and keeps us safe.

RESPONSE:
Lord, thank You for loving me. I need Your protection today as I have been tossed about. Hide me in your arms and keep me safe.

Chapter 37

Psalm 37:4—Delight yourself in the Lord; and He will give you the desires of your heart.

TRUTH:
God created us and knows us better than we know ourselves. We are to rest and relax and enjoy God. God loves us, and He will give us what is best for us in the right time. Will we wait on Him and just delight in Him even when we don't understand?

RESPONSE:
Lord, You know me and my desires. I will rest in You and delight in You and trust that You will give me what is best at the right time.

Chapter 38

Psalm 38:21—Do not forsake me, O Lord; O my God, do not be far from me!

TRUTH:
In the midst of our hurt and distress, we cry out to God. Have we reached the place where we are desperate for Him and Him alone? Do we rely on Him to work in our lives? If we don't, we're finished!

RESPONSE:
O Lord, be near to me and show Yourself to me. Intervene in my life for without You, I am finished!

Chapter 39

Psalm 39:1—I said, "I will guard my ways that I may not sin with my tongue; I will guard my mouth as with a muzzle while the wicked are in my presence."

TRUTH:
The tongue has such power and influence. That power and influence can be used in positive ways. Or, it can get us into a great amount of trouble and cause a lot of problems if we are not guarding what we say. We must control our tongue.

RESPONSE:
Lord, help me to be careful about what I speak and say today. I want to glorify You in every word that I speak.

Chapter 40

Psalm 40:11—You, O Lord, will not withhold Your compassion from me; Your lovingkindness and Your truth will continually preserve me.

TRUTH:
What gives us the strength to make it through each day? God's love and God's truth! Are we relying on those to get through everything that we encounter? Do we study and learn from His truth so that it will sustain us?

RESPONSE:
Father, Your love and truth are amazing, and I pray that You will not withhold them from me. Allow me to know and live in the blessings they provide.

Chapter 41

Psalm 41:9—Even my close friend in whom I trusted, who ate my bread, has lifted up his heel against me.

TRUTH:
At some time, we will feel betrayed by someone close to us. How do we respond? David brought it to God. We must not look to take revenge ourselves, but take our hurt and anger to God for Him to deal with the entire situation. He knows the full story to all situations and is able to defend us when necessary.

RESPONSE:
Lord, help me to respond correctly when I have been hurt and betrayed. Take my hurt and heal it so that only Your feelings of forgiveness remain.

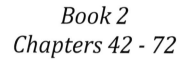

Book 2
Chapters 42 - 72

Chapter 42

Psalm 42:1—As the deer pants for the water brooks, so my soul pants for You, O God.

TRUTH:
Do we long for and seek after God like He is the only thing that matters? Do we cling to Him as though we are desperate and desolate without Him? God knows how much we need Him in our everyday life. Do we recognize our need and act upon it?

RESPONSE:
Lord, without You I am nothing. I cling to You desperately. I need You and desire You today!

Chapter 43

Psalm 43:5—Why are you in despair, O my soul? And why are you disturbed within me? Hope in God, for I shall again praise Him, the help of my countenance and my God.

TRUTH:
Whenever we face problems and difficulties, our hope is found in God. We can praise Him even through the hard times. Are we focusing on God through the difficulties?

RESPONSE:
Lord, no matter how I feel or what downcast thoughts I have, You are my hope. I will praise You today.

Chapter 44

Psalm 44:1—O God, we have heard with our ears, our fathers have told us the work that You did in their days, in the days of old.

TRUTH:
We are responsible for sharing the story of how God works in our lives with our children and others. This doesn't mean just a telling them of God's greatness, but explaining how we know of God's greatness because of the difficulties God has helped us overcome. If we can't share our shortcomings and God's triumphs with our children, they will never fully understand the power and grace of God we tell them about.

RESPONSE:
Lord, help me to be real with my children and with others so they will truly understand Your power as You have worked in my life through both the good times and the bad.

Chapter 45

Psalm 45:17—I will cause Your name to be remembered in all generations; therefore the peoples will give You thanks forever and ever.

TRUTH:
As we look forward to the time when Christ will be set in His position as ruler over everything, we see how God has prepared all to remember and give thanks for Jesus Christ. Are we praising and thanking God now for the position He already holds, but will one day display to the world?

RESPONSE:
Lord, I know that You are over all things and one day that will be displayed to the world. Help me to praise You today in a way that You deserve!

Chapter 46

Psalm 46:1—God is our refuge and strength, a very present help in trouble.

TRUTH:
God is so many things to us: our strength, our refuge, our help. No matter what we are facing, God is present with us in the midst of it. Do we trust in His guiding presence, even when we can't feel Him?

RESPONSE:
Lord, You are present with me in the midst of everything I go through. Lord, help me trust in this presence even when I can't feel it.

Chapter 47

Psalm 47:8—God reigns over the nations, God sits on His holy throne.

TRUTH:
Sometimes, in the midst of all the chaos around us, we forget that God has never left His throne. God is always in control, and He is always on the throne. Do we focus too much on our circumstances or do we stay focused on the truth that God is over all?

RESPONSE:
Lord, help me not to be distracted today by my circumstances. Instead, I choose to trust that You are over everything, because You are!

Chapter 48

Psalm 48:14—For such is God, our God forever and ever; He will guide us until death.

TRUTH:
This psalm describes many attributes of God and with all of them, He is intent on guiding us. He directs us even when we cannot see Him and even when we think we don't want Him to. He directs us all the way up until He leads us home with Him. Do we look for and follow His leading every day?

RESPONSE:
Lord, lead me and guide me today to bring me closer to You. I will follow.

Chapter 49

Psalm 49:7—No man can by any means redeem his brother or give to God a ransom for him.

TRUTH:
We can try and persuade, demonstrate, beg, and plead, but we cannot force someone else into a relationship with God. Each person is responsible to God for his or her relationship with Jesus Christ. We can (and should) pray for them, but we cannot do it for them.

RESPONSE:
Lord, please continue to work in the lives of the others I know who still need You. I pray You will show them their need of You since only You can save them, but they must come to the decision on their own.

Chapter 50

Psalm 50:12b—for the world is Mine, and all it contains.

TRUTH:
Sometimes we think we are supposed to give things to God, In truth, He already owns it. We are to simply acknowledge His ownership and allow Him to do whatever He chooses with it. Do we get angry with God about how He chooses to use His things? Once we truly understand His ownership, we recognize He has every right to do with His things as He pleases.

RESPONSE:
Lord, I pray You will use Your possessions however You see fit. Help me to be willing to give and share as You direct.

Chapter 51

Psalm 51:12—restore to me the joy of Your salvation and sustain me with a willing spirit.

TRUTH:
We can lose our joy, or at least lose the ability to experience it daily. Sin and unrepentance cloud our ability to clearly experience all that God has for us. Repentance restores this joy. Are we lacking joy? We need to repent so that we are restored to the joy that God has given us.

RESPONSE:
Lord, forgive me. I need to be restored to You so I can fully experience Your joy. Without You, there is no joy.

Chapter 52

Psalm 52:2—Your tongue devises destruction, like a sharp razor, O worker of deceit.

TRUTH:
The tongue can be used for great good or great evil, depending on what we choose. When we speak, are we trying to cut others down or are we building them up? The sharpness of the tongue can result in either deceit and destruction or truth and encouragement. How will we use our tongue today?

RESPONSE:
Lord, help me to be faithful to use my tongue today for encouragement and truth.

Chapter 53

Psalm 53:3—Every one of them has turned aside; together they have become corrupt; there is no one who does good, not even one.

TRUTH:
Despite our best efforts, we do not do good. We frequently attempt to be good, but on our own every effort falls short of the standard God has set. The sooner we accept this and beg God's forgiveness, the sooner we can put on God's righteousness and allow Him to be perfection through us.

RESPONSE:
Lord, even when try, I cannot do good apart from You. Work through my every action today to show Your love and mercy to all.

Chapter 54

Psalm 54:4—Behold, God is my helper; The Lord is the sustainer of my soul.

TRUTH:
Sustainer is such a beautiful word. I see a picture of God holding and sheltering a person in one hand while lovingly providing for her needs with the other. The Lord provides us with what we need to be able to keep going even through the darkest times. He sustains us.

RESPONSE:
Lord, it is only through Your provision that I am able to make it through each day. I will trust You to provide what I need for today.

Chapter 55

Psalm 55:22—Cast your burden upon the Lord and He will sustain you; He will never allow the righteous to be shaken.

TRUTH:
God sustains us and holds us firm. But, He will only do that if we cast our burdens on Him. Do we give Him the areas of our life that are worrisome and troublesome? Or, just complain to Him about those areas and never surrender them? We must cast these burdens on Him if we expect to see Him handle them. He will not take them from us, we must lay them down and trust in Him.

RESPONSE:
Lord, You know my burdens today. I give them to You. I know that You are able to take them, and I trust You to deal with these areas completely.

Chapter 56

Psalm 56:11—In God I have put my trust, I shall not be afraid. What can man do to me?

TRUTH:
No matter what we are facing, we can have confidence and faith. We do not have to live in fear. Once we have placed our trust and faith in God, we can be fully assured that He loves us and has a plan for us. No matter what the world does to us, we can confidently hold fast to God knowing that even if the "worst" should happen, we are still held by God.

RESPONSE:
Lord, I do not know what troubles and trials I will face today. But, no matter what this world flings at me, I will hold to You and not be afraid.

Chapter 57

Psalm 57:9—I will give thanks to You, O Lord, among the peoples; I will sing praises to You among the nations.

TRUTH:
We go through so many things in this world, yet regardless of the circumstances we face, we have so much to be thankful for. The Lord has blessed us in so many ways and we are to acknowledge and exalt Him to all people.

RESPONSE:
Lord, I will focus my day today on thankfulness. You are so amazing and have done so many wonderful things in my life. I will share and exalt You with all those I am around today.

Chapter 58

Psalm 58:11—And men will say, "Surely there is a reward for the righteous; Surely there is a God who judges the earth!"

TRUTH:
God is just, and He will judge all. We may not know when God will bring His reward to those who follow Him, but we can be assured that He will. Men will see and will know that God is just and rewards the righteous and punishes the wicked.

RESPONSE:
Lord, I may not know when You will bring about Your justice, but I will live today knowing that one day it will come. Through You, help me to live today in a way that You will reward in Your perfect time.

Chapter 59

Psalm 59:9—Because of his strength I will watch for You, for God is my stronghold.

TRUTH:
God is our strength and our refuge. We cannot hope to stand on our own during the trials and difficulties that we encounter each day. Are we waiting and watching for Him every day and relying on His strength, or are we trying to go forward on our own?

RESPONSE:
Lord, Your strength is the only thing strong enough to make it through my day. Forgive me when I rely on my own strength. Teach me to surrender to Your strength today.

Chapter 60

Psalm 60:12—Through God we shall do valiantly and it is He who will tread down our adversaries.

TRUTH:
When we act, are we doing it on our own, or do we allow God to work through us? Only through God are we able to do things valiantly. We must remember that it is He who will tread down our enemies. There is nothing we can do on our own. We must leave it to Him.

RESPONSE:
Lord, I praise You for doing things valiantly. I will wait on You to take care of my adversaries.

Chapter 61

Psalm 61:2—From the end of the earth I call to You when my heart is faint; Lead me to the rock that is higher than I.

TRUTH:
There are days when, regardless of the truth of our relationship with God, we just don't "feel" like we're close to God. On those days when our heart is faint, we must cling to the truth that God is our rock and doesn't move. He is greater than we are and is always there even when we don't "feel" His presence.

RESPONSE:
Lord, thank You for being my rock! No matter how I feel today, I rest in the truth that You hear me when I cry to You and are leading me in Your ways.

Chapter 62

Psalm 62:8—Trust in Him at all times, O people; pour out your heart before Him; God is a refuge for us.

TRUTH:
Do we rely on God during the good times as well as the bad? Do we share with Him our thoughts and feelings, hopes and dreams? He knows them anyway and wants us to hope and trust in Him alone. Are things going wonderfully in life? Trust in God. Are we almost at the point of giving up? Trust in God. He is our shelter and refuge.

RESPONSE:
Lord, my life is like a roller coaster; some days are great, others are difficult. No matter what today brings, I will trust in You.

Chapter 63

Psalm 63:8—My soul clings to You; Your right hand upholds me.

TRUTH:
This verse brings to mind the picture of a baby animal, like a monkey, that clings desperately to his mother while she moves where they both need to go. We are to cling tightly to God and while we are holding Him, He holds us to Himself as well. Then we simply go with Him wherever He desires to take us.

RESPONSE:
Lord, I don't know where You'll choose to take me today, but I will cling to You as tightly as I can.

Chapter 64

Psalm 64:2—Hide me from the secret counsel of evildoers, from the tumult of those who do iniquity

TRUTH:
This world is full of people who are not seeking God's ways, but their own. As believers, we can find ourselves the targets of their rebellion from God. God is faithful even in the midst of these attacks. He hears and understands when we pray and ask to be hidden from their evil plots and plans.

RESPONSE:
Lord, hide me from the evil plots and plans of the enemy. Give me strength and peace to endure the attacks if that is Your will.

Chapter 65

Psalm 65:8—They who dwell in the ends of the earth stand in awe of Your signs; You make the dawn and the sunset shout for joy.

TRUTH:
All of God's creation is a reflection of His glory and majesty. I love the picture of the sunset and sunrise both shouting for joy because God made them. Do we display the same joy at the opportunity to reflect our Creator?

RESPONSE:
Lord, You created me. You cause me to reflect Your glory and majesty. Today I will live out the joy of belonging to You.

Chapter 66

Psalm 66:12—You made men ride over our heads; we went through fire and through water, yet You brought us out into a place of abundance

TRUTH:
God tries and tests us, as it mentions a few verses earlier in this chapter. He allows certain things to be brought into our lives to both teach and to test. However, if we will lean on Him, He will bring us through into a place of abundance in our relationship with Him. Each trial is an opportunity to more fully trust God.

RESPONSE:
Lord, when You allow the difficulties in my life today, I will trust that You will bring me through. You alone are able to make it through the trials You've given me and I will lean on You.

Chapter 67

Psalm 67:7—God blesses us, that all the ends of the earth may fear Him.

TRUTH:
Why do we receive blessings from the Lord? Is it because we deserve them or have earned them? No, the Lord blesses us for one simple reason: to show His glory and power to all people. When God blesses us, do we share the story or the blessing with others, or do we hoard it all ourselves?

RESPONSE:
Father, You have so richly blessed me in so many ways. Today, help me to use the blessings You've given me to show and teach others about You.

Chapter 68

Psalm 68:1—Let God arise, let His enemies be scattered, and let those who hate Him flee before Him.

TRUTH:
God is powerful and mighty. He will vanquish all His enemies and they will be scattered from His presence. Are we living each day knowing that He will be victorious? Are we anxiously looking forward to that day? Our lives should reflect the confidence we have in the truth of God's victory, as we seek to warn others who have not yet become followers of God.

RESPONSE:
Lord, Your majesty and glory are over everything and one day all will see it. Help me to share You with as many as possible so they may not be scattered or flee from You.

Chapter 69

Psalm 69:13—But as for me, my prayer is to You, O Lord, at an acceptable time; O God, in the greatness of Your lovingkindness, answer me with Your saving truth.

TRUTH:
God hears our prayers and His truth is the answer. Through His lovingkindness and mercy, the Creator of the universe hears us when we pray. No matter what we are facing, His truth is the answer. Do we bring our concerns to Him and seek out His truth to guide us?

RESPONSE:
Father, it is amazing that You hear me when I pray. I will seek out Your truth in response to every situation I encounter today.

Chapter 70

Psalm 70:4—Let all who seek You rejoice and be glad in You; and let those who love Your salvation say continually, "Let God be magnified."

TRUTH:
As we seek after God, we learn and know more about Him. As we know God more, we can't help but rejoice and praise Him for who He is. Are we seeking to know God more? If so, it will be evident by our praise of Him.

RESPONSE:
Lord, You are amazing and wonderful. I will seek You with all my heart and tell of Your greatness throughout the earth.

Chapter 71

Psalm 71:18—And even when I am old and gray, O God, do not forsake me, until I declare Your strength to this generation, Your power to all who are to come.

TRUTH:
No matter our age, God is with us. No matter our age, we have a purpose. We are to declare God and all His strength and glory to the next generation. Do our lives speak of God's glory to those who will come after us?

RESPONSE:
Lord, thank You for Your presence and strength in my life, no matter my age. Help me to leave a legacy of pointing people to You.

Chapter 72

Psalm 72:19—And blessed be His glorious name forever; And may the whole earth be filled with His glory. Amen, and Amen.

TRUTH:
The world is the Lord's and all that is in it. No matter the place or the area, God's name will be blessed. His glory will one day shine throughout every area of the world. Are we praying for and looking forward to that day?

RESPONSE:
Lord, today may Your name be blessed and may the whole earth be filled with Your glory for all to see.

Book 3
Chapters 73 - 89

Chapter 73

Psalm 73:3—For I was envious of the arrogant as I saw the prosperity of the wicked.

TRUTH:
Often we look around our world and it seems like those who do evil are the ones who prosper. We can find ourselves envious of their seeming success. Yet this psalm goes on to detail the fact that God is over all and He will judge all things rightly in the end.

RESPONSE:
Lord, help me to keep my focus on You today and not get distracted by the people around me and their seeming success. I pray You will help me to seek only after You, knowing that if I am seeking You, I am completely successful.

Chapter 74

Psalm 74:16—Yours is the day, Yours also is the night; You have prepared the light and the sun.

TRUTH:
This chapter goes through and details the power and glory of God. He is over each and every day and night. He is in control of all things. Do we follow Him? Do we give Him control of our lives since He is over all things anyway?

RESPONSE:
Father, You are already Lord of today and tonight. I surrender to You and ask You to be over my life during this day You created.

Chapter 75

Psalm 75:9—But as for me, I will declare it forever; I will sing praises to the God of Jacob.

TRUTH:
The Lord's glory and majesty do not change. They are constant, no matter the circumstances, person, or position. Regardless of what we go through, we can sing praise to God because we choose to acknowledge Him. He is worthy of all praise, no matter what.

RESPONSE:
Father, I lift You up and praise Your name. No matter my circumstances, no matter what others around me do, I will praise You.

Chapter 76

Psalm 76:11—Make vows to the Lord your God and fulfill them; Let all who are around Him bring gifts to Him who is to be feared.

TRUTH:
Our relationship with God is just that, a relationship. We are to fulfill our commitments to Him and cherish Him even more than we would any other person. God loves us and basks in our praise of Him, and He is saddened and disappointed when we let Him down. What will we bring to Him to today?

RESPONSE:
Father, today I want to show You my love for You through my actions. I pray that all I do today will reflect Your amazing love for me.

Chapter 77

Psalm 77:9 & 19—Has God forgotten to be gracious? Or has He in anger withdrawn His compassion...? Your way was in the sea and Your paths in mighty waters, and Your footprints may not be known.

TRUTH:
When we experience tragic events we can often find ourselves wondering this very thing. Has God forgotten us? However, even though we can't always see God moving, He is there. No matter what we're facing, God is with us and will walk with us through it.

RESPONSE:
Lord, You are there even when I do not see You. Thank You for Your presence and compassion even in the midst of the most difficult times.

Chapter 78

Psalm 78:4—We will not conceal them from their children, but tell to the generation to come the praises of the Lord, and His strength and His wondrous works that He has done

TRUTH:
One of our great responsibilities is to educate the next generation. More important than math and reading, are we educating our children about the one true God and the amazing things that He has done for us?

RESPONSE:
Lord, help me to be always looking for opportunities to share You and Your faithfulness with not only my own children, but with any other children I come into contact with. I want the next generation to hear about You so they will know You more.

Chapter 79

Psalm 79:9—Help us, O God of our salvation; for the glory of Your name; and deliver us and forgive our sins for Your name's sake.

TRUTH:
God is the one who brings about our deliverance and salvation. Why? Not because we've earned it or deserved it, but because of His name's sake and for His glory. Do we bring glory to God daily for His salvation?

RESPONSE:
Lord, You are the only one worthy of glory and honor. Today, may You receive all the glory for saving me through Your Son Jesus Christ.

Chapter 80

Psalm 80:19—O Lord God of hosts restore us; cause Your face to shine upon us, and we will be saved.

TRUTH:
We cannot fix ourselves. No matter what situation we find ourselves in, we cannot bring about the change we need. Only God can affect lasting change and restoration in our lives. We must stop trying to make things better on our own and start surrendering to the only One who can.

RESPONSE:
Lord, I can't fix all the things in my life that are broken. Instead, today I give them to You. Restore me.

Chapter 81

Psalm 81:13—Oh that My people would listen to Me, that Israel would walk in My ways!

TRUTH:
God is speaking in this verse and sharing His longing and desire for His people. God longs for us to turn to Him. His heart aches for us to follow in His ways. He wants what is best for us, and He knows that what is best is found in following His ways.

RESPONSE:
Lord, help me to long for You as much as You long for me. I pray You will help me listen to You and walk in Your ways because I love You.

Chapter 82

Psalm 82:4—Rescue the weak and needy, deliver them out of the hand of the wicked.

TRUTH:
Even when we feel the weakest and most alone, God is there. He is our deliverer. He is our rescuer. He will take us out of the hand of whatever we are facing and will hold us in His hand.

RESPONSE:
Lord, it doesn't matter what I feel, You are my deliverer. I will trust in Your hand to hold me through everything I encounter today.

Chapter 83

Psalm 83:3—They make shrewd plans against Your people, and conspire together against Your treasured ones.

TRUTH:
As followers of Jesus, people will not necessarily like us. In fact, we have an enemy, Satan, who will use people to stir up trouble and plan evil to happen to us. God does not leave us alone, and He will one day set things completely right and just. Even through it all, we are His treasured ones. We are to trust in Him no matter what anyone else does.

RESPONSE:
Father, I lift up Your plans to You. Keep me focused on You and Your designs for me no matter what shrewd and evil plan Satan brings against me.

Chapter 84

Psalm 84:5—How blessed is the man whose strength is in You, in whose heart are the highways to Zion!

TRUTH:
If we allow Christ to be our strength, then we will be blessed through Him. Even more than that, do we hold in our hearts a desire for the peace and the power of Christ to be displayed through our lives? In our heart of hearts is that our motivation? We need both the desire and the strength in order to lead people in the way of Christ.

RESPONSE:
Father, You know my heart. You know my desire to lead others to a deeper relationship with You. Bless me with Your strength and Your path to lead people in Your way.

Chapter 85

Psalm 85:2—You forgave the iniquity of Your people; You covered all their sin.

TRUTH:
When we mess up, God forgives us. He covers our sin. He longs to have us restored to Him. He doesn't want us to stand in our sin. Do we sit and wallow in our own self-pity and guilt? Or instead, do we accept God's forgiveness and work to show Him we love Him by obeying Him from that point on?

RESPONSE:
Lord, I pray that You will rescue me out of sin and cover me. I am Yours, and I want to display Your forgiveness for all people.

Chapter 86

Psalm 86:11—Teach me Your way O Lord; I will walk in Your truth; Unite my heart to fear Your name.

TRUTH:
The Lord is the best teacher to show us how to walk in His way. I want to be an eager student to learn and do all that He has for me. I want whatever it takes for my heart to be united in its desire to fear and worship God. Does this describe your desire today?

RESPONSE:
Father, teach me so that I walk in Your truth. Join me to You. Help my heart to not be divided over the silly things of this world, but to be united to You.

Chapter 87

Psalm 87:7—Then those who sing as well as those who play the flutes shall say, "All my springs of joy are in You."

TRUTH:
We are to rejoice and demonstrate our love for God and our joy in Him. The Lord is the one who gives joy in every circumstance we face. The Lord is over all.

RESPONSE:
Father, no matter what comes my way, all my springs of joy are in You. I praise You and ask that You help me share that joy with others today.

Chapter 88

Psalm 88:13—But I, O Lord, have cried out to You for help, and in the morning my prayer comes before You.

TRUTH:
In the darkest times, in the pits of life, when we cannot possibly believe there is a way out, God is there. He still hears our cry even when we don't feel like we're being heard. Our prayers come before Him as He leads us to go through the valleys of life.

RESPONSE:
Lord, even in the pits of life, You are with me and hear my cries. You love me and no matter what I am walking through today, I know You are with me.

Chapter 89

Psalm 89:15—How blessed are the people who know the joyful sound! O Lord, they walk in the light of Your countenance.

TRUTH:
With all that we hear each day, do we know how to recognize the joyful sound of the Lord? Can we identify Him working and moving in our life each day? Knowing Him and recognizing His moving in our life daily gives us joy and blessing. It allows us to walk in the light of His countenance, not the darkness of our own.

RESPONSE:
Lord, even when my world looks dark, You are moving and working. Help me to see Your fingerprints on my life today and walk in Your light.

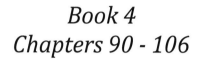

Book 4
Chapters 90 - 106

Chapter 90

Psalm 90:12—So teach us to number our days, that we may present to You a heart of wisdom.

TRUTH:
Often it can be easy to forget that our time on this earth is numbered. We won't live forever. God indicates that we are wise to keep that in mind and to "number our days." Only by maintaining the proper perspective can we truly have a heart of wisdom.

RESPONSE:
Lord, I know that my time here is limited. Help me to use my time to do and be a part of things that please and honor You, for that is the only wise use of the time You've provided me.

Chapter 91

Psalm 91:15—"He will call upon Me and I will answer him; I will be with him in trouble; I will rescue him and honor him."

TRUTH:
God doesn't promise us that we won't have trouble. He does promise that He will be with us in the trouble. He will answer us when we call on Him. He will honor and rescue us. Do we trust Him and call on Him through every situation we encounter, good or bad?

RESPONSE:
Father, no matter what I face today, You are with me. I will call to You and wait for You as You walk with me through the trouble.

Chapter 92

Psalm 92:4—For You, O Lord, have made me glad by what You have done. I will sing for joy at the works of Your hands.

TRUTH:
God is amazing and wonderful. He does incredible and awesome things. Even when we do not understand what He is doing or why, we can take heart in knowing that God will always be who He is. Because of this, I will have joy and share that joy with others.

RESPONSE:
Lord, I thank You for all the wonderful ways You work in my life. I pray You will help me to share Your joy in all circumstances today.

Chapter 93

Psalm 93:1—The Lord reigns, He is clothed with majesty; The Lord has clothed and girded Himself with strength; indeed the world is firmly established, it will not be moved.

TRUTH:
The Lord is over all. Not only does He have that position, but He has clothed Himself in such a way that His position is unmistakable and everything points to it. The qualities mentioned: strength and majesty, they are not just things God has, but things He is. We can never know true strength and majesty apart from God.

RESPONSE:
Lord, You are over all. I praise You for Your amazing character and position. Help me to rely on You in all areas today and display Your majesty and strength to everyone.

Chapter 94

Psalm 94:19—When my anxious thoughts multiply within me, Your consolations delight my soul.

TRUTH:
God is our help and our comfort. When anxious thoughts come, and they will come, He is the one to calm, reassure, and impart peace. Are we willing to turn to the one who delights our soul during the times when we are anxious and fearful?

RESPONSE:
Lord, I want to bask in the delight You bring to my soul. I pray You will help me to turn over to You all my anxious thoughts.

Chapter 95

Psalm 95:4-5—In whose hand are the depths of the earth, the peaks of the mountains are His also. The sea is His, for it was He who made it, and His hands formed the dry land.

TRUTH:
No matter where we are, we're surrounded by God's creation. He is everywhere and in everything. We give Him praise for being in everything, over everything, and the creator of everything.

RESPONSE:
Lord, I know that You are over everything. I pray that You will help me to see all that You are in today and all that You created today. Lord, You are evident in all Your creation.

Chapter 96

Psalm 96:3—Tell of His glory among the nations, His wonderful deeds among all the peoples.

TRUTH:
Yes, we know that God is amazing and wonderful, but do we share it with others? Do we actively look for opportunities to tell of His glory and wonderful deeds? While we must each come to the place where we make an individual decision about our relationship with God, that doesn't mean we are to be silent and private about it. We must tell!

RESPONSE:
Lord, it can be easy to just know the truth of Your majesty, but not share it regularly. I pray that today Your glory and deeds will be on my lips quickly and often.

Chapter 97

Psalm 97:7—Let all those be ashamed who serve graven images, who boast themselves of idols; worship Him, all you gods.

TRUTH:
Do we give anything a higher priority than God? Anything we place above God has become an idol and can include such things as money, security, popularity, or success, among many others. These things are not wrong by themselves, but pursuing them above God will lead to our shame. All these other things will eventually bow down and worship the one true God.

RESPONSE:
Lord, let nothing come between me and You. I want to love and serve You only.

Chapter 98

Psalm 98:2—The Lord has made known His salvation; He has revealed His righteousness in the sight of the nations.

TRUTH:
God is not trying to keep secrets from us to be mysterious. He wants us to know Him and His salvation. Sometimes we try to make God seem more complicated than He is. God has revealed His righteousness to the nations, are we looking for it? Do we recognize God at work when we see it?

RESPONSE:
Lord, You are working to reveal Your will and Yourself to people. Help me to see You each day and to learn more about You each day.

Chapter 99

Psalm 99:6—Moses and Aaron were among His priests, and Samuel was among those who call on His name; They called upon the Lord and He answered them.

TRUTH:
God is the same yesterday, today, and forever. He is the same God that Moses, Aaron, and Samuel all called to. He has not changed. He has not aged. He has the same character and the same power and the same desires now that He had then. We can look back through the Bible and know that as God responded to others, He will for us as well.

RESPONSE:
Lord, thank You for the examples through the Bible so we can have faith that You are the same for us as You were for others.

Chapter 100

Psalm 100:2—Serve the Lord with gladness; come before Him with joyful singing.

TRUTH:
Are we excited about coming into God's presence? Do we celebrate each moment we spend in front of the throne of God? Do we realize that every day God wants to meet with us and share with us? God wants an intimate relationship with us and we have the opportunity to come before the Creator of the Universe. Do we display our joy in this relationship for others to see?

RESPONSE:
Lord, You are amazing and I love You. With gladness and joy I will do anything and everything You ask of me. I praise You for who You are!

Chapter 101

Psalm 101:7—He who practices deceit shall not dwell within my house; He who speaks falsehood shall not maintain his position before me.

TRUTH:
What type of company do we keep? Who do we allow to influence and guide us? Are these people following God or not? We need to be around non-believers in order to influence them and display Christ to them, but in turn we are to be careful of the influence they have in our life.

RESPONSE:
Father, help me evaluate every relationship that I have. I pray that You will show me any relationships in my life that are not where You want them to be so I can change them to glorify You.

Chapter 102

Psalm 102:2—Do not hide Your face from me in the day of my distress; Incline Your ear to me; In the day when I call answer me quickly.

TRUTH:
In the times when we go through difficulties and trials, God is there. We can rest in that truth, even when all else around us doesn't seem that way. We are able to call out to God in the midst of these times, and He hears us. He is there, no matter how it feels to us at the time.

RESPONSE:
God, I know the truth that You are there. You never leave and never forsake me. Even in those days when I don't feel Your presence, You are there. When I go through hard times and trials, You will be there. I will trust in You.

Chapter 103

Psalm 103:10—He has not dealt with us according to our sins, nor rewarded us according to our iniquities.

TRUTH:
Often, we think we deserve certain things in life, or that God owes us something. Thankfully, God does not immediately give us what we deserve. He is merciful and patient and has made a way for forgiveness of our sins. Only if we DON'T request His merciful gift of salvation does He eventually give us exactly what we as sinners truly deserve: an eternity of judgment

RESPONSE:
Lord, thank You so much for not giving me what I as a sinner deserve, but for making a way for me to come to You. I pray You will help me to never overlook all that You have saved me from: the direct consequences of my sin.

Chapter 104

Psalm 104:33—I will sing to the Lord as long as I live; I will sing praise to my God while I have my being.

TRUTH:
This psalm praises God for His creation. As part of His creation, we sing back our praise to Him for everything that we are. He alone is worthy. He alone is mighty. He alone created me and loves me exactly as I am.

RESPONSE:
Lord, I will praise You with all that I am. I praise You for all that I am. You are worthy of all my praise!

Chapter 105

Psalm 105:3—Glory in His holy name, let the heart of those who seek the Lord be glad.

TRUTH:
The Lord is holy and His name is holy. Seeking Him, we find joy. Are we seeking after the holy name of Jesus? Is our heart glad? If not, we need to reevaluate what we are seeking after.

RESPONSE:
Lord, I want You and You only. I pray that You will help me seek You at all times in my life, especially today.

Chapter 106

Psalm 106:8—Nevertheless He saved them for the sake of His name, that He might make His power known.

TRUTH:
As this psalm recounts the entire history of the Israelite people, it tells of all that God has done for them. Why did God save them? He saved them for the sake of His own name. That is why He offers salvation to us. That is why He does the things that He does, for the sake of His name. Do we do everything for the purpose of pointing people to Christ and glorifying His name?

RESPONSE:
Lord, I thank You for all that You have done for me, and I praise You for all that You have done. Thank You for being worthy of the praise Your name deserves.

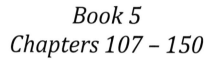

Book 5
Chapters 107 – 150

Chapter 107

Psalm 107:9—For He has satisfied the thirsty soul, and the hungry soul He has filled with what is good.

TRUTH:
God is the fulfillment of all our needs and desires. Do we yearn for Him like our body craves food and drink? He is the only thing that will completely satisfy our every longing and desire.

RESPONSE:
Father, I long for You. I need You and I desire You more than food, drink, or even air. I know only You can satisfy the longings of my heart. I will cling to You and only You for everything.

Chapter 108

Psalm 108:12—Oh give us help against the adversary, for deliverance by man is in vain.

TRUTH:
As David sang through this psalm, he knew that no matter what battle he faced, God is the one who brings victory. What battles are we going through? Only God brings the victory. Having friends stand by us and help us is great and certainly needed, but we must trust and wait on God to bring the victory.

RESPONSE:
Lord, we praise You for all that You are. You are victorious. You are above all and through You we find help and deliverance in all things.

Chapter 109

Psalm 109:4—In return for my love they act as my accusers; but I am in prayer.

TRUTH:
We have all been let down or betrayed by people. David was no exception. How did he respond? He brought it to the Lord in prayer? He didn't hold back his feelings of frustration from God, but he didn't act on them. He allowed God to handle the situation. Do we express our frustration to God, or instead do we share with everyone around us? Do we allow God to deal with the situation we are experiencing?

RESPONSE:
Lord, I will bring my frustration and feelings of betrayal to You. You know how I feel, and I will trust You to deal with all situations and the people involved. I place my complete trust in You.

Chapter 110

Psalm 110:2—The Lord will stretch forth Your strong scepter from Zion, saying, "Rule in the midst of Your enemies."

TRUTH:
Jesus Christ is the Messiah. He quoted from this psalm as He explained Himself to others. He will stretch forth His scepter and will rule the entire earth, regardless of who believes in Him or not. The truth of Jesus' reign is not affected by our opinion of it.

RESPONSE:
Lord, You are indeed over all in this world and You will rule over all. I thank You for all that You are and I praise You for Your truth.

Chapter 111

Psalm 111:9—He has sent redemption to His people; He has ordained His covenant forever; Holy and awesome is His name.

TRUTH:
This psalm is a beautiful listing of praise for all that God does. He has provided a means of salvation that will be in place forever. He is truly awesome and amazing. Have we stopped to praise Him for all the amazing things He's done in our life as well as in the lives of others?

RESPONSE:
Lord, You are truly wonderful. You have done so many things for me and I don't always tell You how thankful I am. I praise You for all You do.

Chapter 112

Psalm 112:7—He will not fear evil tidings; His heart is steadfast, trusting in the Lord.

TRUTH:
Do we spend our time worrying about what may come? Are we more focused on the possibilities of problems than on our trust in God? God is there; He is in control. There is nothing that will happen that He doesn't already know and have the answer to. We can trust in Him and place our heart in His hand. We don't have to be consumed by worry about the "what if." We can remember, "no matter what, God."

RESPONSE:
Lord, no matter what comes today, You are still in control. I will not fear the "what ifs," but I will completely rest in You. Help me to let go of my worry and anxiety and relax in Your steadfast love.

Chapter 113

Psalm 113:5—Who is like the Lord our God, who is enthroned on high?

TRUTH:
Lots of religions are out there and they all claim many things about their "gods." However, only God is the true God. Only He is the one enthroned on high. Only He has the power, majesty, and awesomeness that is true of God. Only He is. Do we recognize the amazingness of God and then also see that He wants to have a personal relationship with us?

RESPONSE:
Lord, You are the alpha and the omega. You are over everything and above all. You are the creator of all things. Lord, I will worship and follow You. You have made me Your child through Jesus Christ, and I will love and adore You.

Chapter 114

Psalm 114:7—Tremble, O earth, before the Lord; before the God of Jacob.

TRUTH:
God is not just the Lord of all mankind, He is God over all things, including the earth, the rocks, the seas, and the trees. All of His creation knows and bows down before its creator. Do we have the same level of worship for God that the rest of creation has?

RESPONSE:
Lord, I also tremble before You. You are amazing and wonderful. You're perfect and powerful. You are my Creator and Savior and, like the whole earth, I worship You.

Chapter 115

Psalm 115:1—Not to us, O Lord, not to us, but to Your name give glory because of Your lovingkindness, because of Your truth.

TRUTH:
Do we spend our time waiting and hoping for God to glorify us? Are we expecting for God to make us famous or well-known? The truth is that we should desire only for God to be glorified through our life and actions. God is the one who is worthy of the praise and honor, not us.

RESPONSE:
Father, may You work through me today to bring glory to Yourself, not to me. I am not deserving of praise or honor, only You. Apart from You, I can do nothing.

Chapter 116

Psalm 116:6—The Lord preserves the simple; I was brought low, and He saved me.

TRUTH:
It can be easy to think, "I'm not smart enough," or, "I'm not pretty enough," or whatever; but God knows exactly who we are and what we've done. He created us and He loves us. He wants us to trust in Him through the good times and the difficult times. He lifts us up and He saves us.

RESPONSE:
Lord, I am simply Yours. I have nothing else to boast about and nothing to offer. Yet You love me and save me from the depths of my own sin.

Chapter 117

Psalm 117:1—Praise the Lord, all nations; Laud Him all peoples!

TRUTH:
The Lord is worthy of praise from all people, everywhere. Do we seek to share His name and His glory around the world? God loves the whole world and desires them to know and receive His love.

RESPONSE:
Lord, it's easy to only focus on myself and what I can see right around me. I pray You will open my eyes to the truth of Your love for the whole world and all the peoples of the world.

Chapter 118

Psalm 118:6—The Lord is for me; I will not fear; What can man do to me?

TRUTH:
No matter what we're going through, God is with us and is for us. We do not have to be afraid of circumstances. We simply have to trust in Him and continue to be obedient. There is nothing that a man can do to us that God cannot work through for His glory and purpose.

RESPONSE:
Lord, You are my protection and security. No matter what happens, I know that You are in control and I trust in You without fear.

Chapter 119

Psalm 119:41-42—May Your loving-kindnesses also come to me, O Lord, Your salvation according to Your word; So I will have an answer for him who reproaches me, for I trust in Your word.

TRUTH:

What is one reason God showers us with His lovingkindnesses and salvation? He does it so we will have an answer for those who are against us. We trust in the word of God and through His word, He supplies all we need, including the answers for those who come against us. Do we respond in lovingkindness to those who come against us? Through Christ and His word, we can.

RESPONSE:

Lord, I love Your word. Through Your word I learn how to respond to every situation. I pray Your lovingkindness will show through my every action and word today, no matter the situation or circumstance.

Chapter 120

Psalm 120:2—Deliver my soul, O Lord, from lying lips, from a deceitful tongue.

TRUTH:
Have we ever been lied about? Have others ever spoken falsely about us? In this psalm, the author is asking God to deliver him from such people and their lies. Do we rely on God to address these situations or do we just try to get back at the person? We are to take our concerns about our attackers to God and allow Him to deliver us.

RESPONSE:
Father, You are bigger than those who would try to say evil about me. I know You are truth, and I will rest in You and allow You to respond.

Chapter 121

Psalm 121:2—My help comes from the Lord, who made heaven and earth

TRUTH:
What a beautiful statement of complete trust in God! No matter what we are going through, our help comes from the Lord. Our help comes from the very One who created the entire heavens and earth. I can trust in, not just a president or king, friend or relative, but in the founder and creator of everything. I can trust in the person who made something from nothing. He is my help, and I will trust in Him.

RESPONSE:
Father, I can never thank You enough for all You have helped me through. I pray You will lead me to trust You completely in all areas of my life.

Chapter 122

Psalm 122:1—I was glad when they said to me, "Let us go to the house of the Lord."

TRUTH:
Do we look forward to meeting with God and with our fellow believers? Are we excited about sharing with Him and learning from Him together? Going to the house of God is a beautiful chance to not only set aside time for God, but to also meet with others who share our joy. Having Jesus in our hearts allows us to meet with God every minute of every day. Do we seek Him as diligently and with such joy?

RESPONSE:
Lord, I am glad when I get to go meet with You and other believers, but I am equally glad when I get to just meet with You. I desire to have You as the guiding force of every minute of my day today.

Chapter 123

Psalm 123:2—Behold, as the eyes of servants look to the hand of their master, as the eyes of a maid to the hand of her mistress, so our eyes look to the Lord our God, until He is gracious to us.

TRUTH:
God provides everything for us. We are to trust Him for everything we need. Just like a servant is completely dependent on their master for everything they have, we are dependent on God for everything we have. We can hold on to Him and trust Him until He supplies our needs as promised. Do we wait on Him and trust Him to provide exactly what we need?

RESPONSE:
Lord, I love You and serve You with gladness. I will come to You with all my concerns and I will wait on You. Lord, You are my supplier and I will be content with what You supply as You know my every need.

Chapter 124

Psalm 124:7—Our soul has escaped as a bird out of the snare of the trapper; the snare is broken and we have escaped.

TRUTH:
This entire psalm speaks of the Lord's deliverance from those who are seeking to destroy us. We have an enemy who seeks our destruction. He will use whatever means he can to try and trap us. But we have a Savior who delivers us, if we will trust in Him. He breaks us free from everything that seeks our destruction. Are we living today knowing we are free from the destroyer?

RESPONSE:
Lord, I love You and I trust in Your deliverance. Because of You I am free and I trust in You for all things today.

Chapter 125

Psalm 125:2—As the mountains surround Jerusalem, so the Lord surrounds His people from this time forth and forever.

TRUTH:
God surrounds us with His protection, with His love, and with everything that He is. He will not be shaken and will not be moved. The Lord is over all and in all. He is trustworthy and reliable. Do we place our trust in Him no matter what?

RESPONSE:
Lord, You are surrounding and protecting me at this very moment. I pray You will help me rely only on You in all circumstances.

Chapter 126

Psalm 126:5-6—Those who sow in tears shall reap with joyful shouting. He who goes to and fro weeping, carrying his bag of seed, shall indeed come again with a shout of joy bringing his sheaves with him.

TRUTH:
The Lord's timing is perfect, yet often we do not understand it. This verse doesn't mean that we should go about crying all the time, but it does mean that we will hurt at times. We will face disappointment and loss. Yet, God is there through it all and He knows the perfect timing for all things. We can have joy even through the pain knowing that God is bringing about His results in His timing; and His results are always cause for shouts of joy!

RESPONSE:
Lord, take the tears and the sorrows and the hurts. Sow them with Your love and understanding and timing so that I may have Your joy no matter what happens, knowing that Your harvest is always better than my plans.

Chapter 127

Psalm 127:1—Unless the Lord builds the house, they labor in vain who build it; Unless the Lord guards the city, the watchman keeps awake in vain.

TRUTH:
All our plans, all our works, if they are not led by God, they are pointless and meaningless. It's not enough to simply ask God to bless the work that we are already doing. We must be following along with God's work in the first place. Are we allowing God to direct and build in our lives, or are we working in vain?

RESPONSE:
Father, I only want Your works and Your plans. I surrender all the plans I've tried myself and I pray for Your work and Your work only to be done.

Chapter 128

Psalm 128:2—When you shall eat of the fruit of your hands, you will be happy and it will be well with you.

TRUTH:
Productivity. God made us with purpose. God gave us abilities and the opportunities to use those abilities for Him. We will only be truly happy when we are daily doing the things God intended us to be doing. Are we seeking for and actually doing all that God wants us to be doing?

RESPONSE:
Lord, I want to do the things You have purposed for me. I relish being able to watch You use me and my abilities to accomplish Your work.

Chapter 129

Psalm 129:2—Many times they have persecuted me from my youth up; Yet they have not prevailed against me.

TRUTH:
We are rarely ever attacked just once. The enemies will generally attack over and over again looking for us to give up, give in, or stumble and fall. Because of Christ, we can say, like the psalmist, that though we've been attacked several times, they have not prevailed against us. Only by resting and relying on Christ can we overcome the many attacks and stay faithful and obedient to Him. Are we relying on Him today? We can be sure the attacks will come.

RESPONSE:
Lord, I will trust You and through Your strength I will stand, no matter what comes against me today. I know that through You no one will prevail against me.

Chapter 130

Psalm 130:5—I wait for the Lord, my soul does wait, and in His word do I hope.

TRUTH:
Waiting is so hard! Most of us have figured out how to avoid waiting or to shorten our wait time for things. God doesn't work that way. We wait for the Lord. He will always move in His own perfect time. But He doesn't leave us alone while we wait. Plus, we have His word. We use His word to remind ourselves of the promises of God and place our trust and hope in Him and His timing.

RESPONSE:
Lord, I don't always understand Your timing, but I will wait for You. I will hope in You because You never leave me alone. I will rest in the promises of Your word!

Chapter 131

Psalm 131:1—O Lord, my heart is not proud, nor my eyes haughty; Nor do I involve myself in great matters, or in things too difficult for me.

TRUTH:
It can be easy to think we are great and wonderful all on our own. In actuality, we are special because God created us and everything we do that is good is because of His grace. We must give God the praise and glory, and be content in His plans. He knows and understands all things, including those things that are too great and difficult for us to understand in the moment.

RESPONSE:
Lord, I know that You are great and over all things. I will remember that You are in control of all things. I will not think I'm over things, but I will wait and trust in You.

Chapter 132

Psalm 132:4-5—I will not give sleep to my eyes or slumber to my eyelids, until I find a place for the Lord, a dwelling place for the Mighty One of Jacob.

TRUTH:
The psalmist remembers the passion and focus that King David had. David wanted to build a dwelling place for God. Are we as passionate about our desire to show God our love and devotion? What area of life stirs us and gives us an unstoppable desire to act out of love for God?

RESPONSE:
Lord, I pray that my love for You would become a passion to act on Your behalf. I pray I will be so focused on my love for You that everything else seems like a waste of my time.

Chapter 133

Psalm 133:1—Behold, how good and how pleasant it is for brothers to dwell together in unity!

TRUTH:
How would people characterize our relationships? Unified? Harmonious? These are the traits that God desires in our relationships with others, especially our brothers in Christ. We are not always going to agree, but for those of us who have asked Jesus Christ to be the Lord of our life, our ultimate goals and desires are to be the same as Christ's, which will lead to unity with other believers. Are we striving for unity with others? Are we focused on God's goals, which bring unity, or on our own, which don't?

RESPONSE:
Lord, help me to focus on You first. You bring unity, not division. I pray You will help me to seek after unity in all my relationships.

Chapter 134

Psalm 134:3—May the Lord bless you from Zion, He who made heaven and earth.

TRUTH:
When we ask for God to bless us, we must remember who He is and what He's done. He is the creator of all things. He is over all. His blessings can be almost anything as He has the ability to be and to move however He wants to. Are we content with God's blessings, whatever they may look like?

RESPONSE:
Lord, You are Creator of all things. You made the heavens and the earth and all things in them. I will praise You and be content with Your blessings, whatever form they take.

Chapter 135

Psalm 135:13—Your name, O Lord, is everlasting; Your remembrance, O Lord, throughout all generations.

TRUTH:
The Lord and His name are permanent and steadfast. They do not change with time. They are not influenced by the happenings of the world. God is God. He is over all things. He lasts throughout all generations. Sharing our knowledge of the Lord and who He is with the next generation is of vital importance. God will be the same for future generations as He is for us now, like He was for our ancestors.

RESPONSE:
Lord, You are forever and everlasting. You are the same from generation to generation. I will share who You are with all people.

Chapter 136

Psalm 136:1—Give thanks to the Lord, for He is good, for is lovingkindness is everlasting.

TRUTH:
In this psalm the phrase, "for His lovingkindness is everlasting" is repeated over and over again. What does God do anything? Because "His lovingkindness is everlasting." Why does God allow hard times? Why does God give us victory over our enemies? Why did God create the world? Why do we give Him thanks? Because His lovingkindness is everlasting!

RESPONSE:
Lord, You are the same yesterday, today, and forever. You are love and everything You do is a result of Your love. I will praise You and thank You in all things because Your lovingkindness is everlasting.

Chapter 137

Psalm 137:6—May my tongue cling to the roof of my mouth if I do not remember you, if I do not exalt Jerusalem above my chief joy.

TRUTH:
This psalm was written while the Israelites were in captivity in Babylon. When they thought back to Jerusalem, the city where the met God and worshiped Him, they longed for that closeness and presence of God like they had in Jerusalem. Do we remember and long for those times in our life when our relationship with God felt close? Are we seeking after that fellowship above all other things?

RESPONSE:
Lord, I long to be close to You and to know You. I will see You above anything else in my life and I pray I will allow nothing to cause me to lose my focus on You.

Chapter 138

Psalm 138:3—On the day I called, You answered me; You made me bold with strength in my soul.

TRUTH:
God hears us when we call. The psalmist indicated that God answered him on the same day. God makes us bold and gives us strength. This boldness and strength goes all the way to our soul. God's strength is not a surface boldness, but it's one that goes all through us.

RESPONSE:
Lord, You answer when I call. You don't leave me alone. You give me strength and boldness that goes all through me. I praise You for always being there for me and for giving me what I need in every situation.

Chapter 139

Psalm 139:14—I will give thanks to You, for I am fearfully and wonderfully made, wonderful are Your works, and my soul knows it very well.

TRUTH:
We are crafted by God. Each and every fiber of our being was knit lovingly in place by the One who knows all. We are each special and unique and God loves us very much. Do we discount the work of God in making us who we are, or do we give Him the praise for each part that is created in His image, even the parts we don't understand or don't like? We are God's workmanship. His workmanship is wonderful, and we are to give Him thanks.

RESPONSE:
Lord, I don't always understand why You made me the way You did, with certain traits and characteristics. Nevertheless, I am Your creation and I will praise You with all that I am and all that You've made me to be. I know that Your creation lines up with Your word and that only those traits which are in line with Your word are from You. I will praise You.

Chapter 140

Psalm 140:4—Keep me, O Lord, from the hands of the wicked. Preserve me from violent men who have purposed to trip up my feet.

TRUTH:
I've heard some people say that it's selfish and wrong to pray for yourself, yet the psalmist does that all the time. In this psalm, he's praying to be rescued and kept safe from evil people intent on destroying his witness. As God's children, He wants to see us, not necessarily safe, but fulfilling our purpose and calling. God has a purpose for us and we are to pray for help to keep us from stumbling and sinning. We need to be kept safe from the wicked so we don't follow in their ways.

RESPONSE:
Lord, while I would like to be kept safe from harm, I'm much more interested in being kept safe from evil. I want to please You and fulfill Your plans for me, not be distracted by evil influences that might cause me to stumble and not follow You.

Chapter 141

Psalm 141:3—Set a guard, O Lord, over my mouth; keep watch over the door of my lips.

TRUTH:
Guarding what we say is a difficult job. In the book of James, he asks who can tame the tongue. The answer is that only God can control our tongues. We must allow Him to be in control of our mouth and the words that come from it. The mouth is such a powerful influence; it is a moment by moment job to keep it obedient to all that God wants. Only through Christ's strength and by allowing Him to guard the mouth, can it be done.

RESPONSE:
Lord, I give You control of my mouth. Use it to say what You want. Keep it silent as You want. I surrender control to You.

Chapter 142

Psalm 142:1-2—I cry aloud with my voice to the Lord; I make supplication with my voice to the Lord. I pour out my complaint before Him; I declare my trouble before Him.

TRUTH:
Many things we encounter and go through are causes for frustration and anger. Who is the first person we voice our complaint to? It should be God. He knows all and hears all. He and He alone is the one we are to voice our concerns to. He then will bring about the people and the opportunities to further share with others, if that is what He would have us do. He knows which situations need to be brought to light. Otherwise, He is sufficient to help us carry our burdens.

RESPONSE:
Lord, so often I get this backward and I take my complaints and frustrations to other people first. Forgive me and help me to realize Your timing is perfect. If I will trust You, You will orchestrate things in a way that will glorify You and work through the problems so much more effectively than I ever could.

Chapter 143

Psalm 143:8—Let me hear Your lovingkindness in the morning; for I trust in You. Teach me the way in which I should walk; for to You I lift up my soul.

TRUTH:
Because sin came into the world and we are born into sin, we do not naturally know how to walk in obedience to God. We must hear of God's truths, we must trust that they are true. We must be taught what is right and how to live it, and ultimately, we must surrender ourselves to God so He can live His truth through us.

RESPONSE:
Lord, I wish I always knew to do what is right, but I don't. I pray You will speak to me and teach me so that I will trust in You and allow You to live through me more and more each day.

Chapter 144

Psalm 144:4—Man is like a mere breath; His days are like a passing shadow.

TRUTH:
Because our senses are so attuned to what we see, hear, and touch around us, it can be easy to lose sight of the fact that our lives here are temporary. God created us as eternal beings that just spend a passing shadow of time on earth. Do we focus on the eternal or do we become focused on gaining "success" in just this shadow of life. We must be reminded that this life is just a breath.

RESPONSE:
Lord, help me to focus today on the eternal. I pray that the choices I make today will be made with eternity in mind, not just what I can easily see, hear, and touch.

Chapter 145

Psalm 145:18—The Lord is near to all who call upon Him, to all who call upon Him in truth.

TRUTH:
No matter what we are going through, if we are calling on the Lord, He is near. There are times when we are walking through difficulties that we do not feel God's presence. However, the truth is that He is near. We can call on God and know that He is near, even when it doesn't feel like it.

RESPONSE:
Lord, no matter what I feel while I am going through difficulties, I will trust the truth that You are near. I praise You for keeping Your promises to me.

Chapter 146

Psalm 146:3—Do not trust in princes, in mortal man, in whom there is no salvation.

TRUTH:
During difficulties and uncertain times, who do we look toward? Who do we place our trust in to get us through? If we are trusting in anything besides God, we will be disappointed. Governments fall, leaders die, friends betray, but only God gives salvation to all who ask of Him.

RESPONSE:
Lord, today, no matter what happens, I pray I will trust only in You. Help me to live out my trust in everything I say and do.

Chapter 147

Psalm 147:5—Great is our Lord and abundant in strength; His understanding is infinite.

TRUTH:
I'm so glad God's understanding is infinite because my understanding is not. At times it seems like there are more things I don't understand than things I do. Things I thought I understood, I find out later that maybe I really didn't. The Lord knows all and understands all. He is able to handle and direct everything that comes. He is not surprised and He is in control.

RESPONSE:
Lord, I don't understand and it's driving me crazy. I want to know and see the big picture in my life. I want to feel in control, but I can't. I surrender these desires to You knowing that You understand and are in control and I can trust in You.

Chapter 148

Psalm 148:13—Let them praise the name of the Lord, for His name alone is exalted; His glory is above earth and heaven.

TRUTH:
Have we praised God today? No matter our circumstance or situation, He is worthy of all praise and honor. He alone is to be exalted, not money, or success, or even our desires. He is the creator of all things and He is over all.

RESPONSE:
Lord, it can be easy to say I praise You and then live praising myself. Let everything I do today be an extension of You and display my praise of You to all people I'm around.

Chapter 149

Psalm 149:4—For the Lord takes pleasure in His people; He will beautify the afflicted ones with salvation.

TRUTH:
As a child of God, we can know that God takes pleasure in us. He also bestows us with beauty through His gift of salvation. We all have days where we don't feel beautiful or pleasing to God, but that doesn't change the fact that He sees us as beautiful and takes pleasure in us.

RESPONSE:
Lord, some days I don't feel pretty or worthy for You to take pleasure in me. Help me to rest in Your truth and not my feelings. I love You, and I love how You love me.

Chapter 150

Psalm 150:6—Let everything that has breath praise the Lord. Praise the Lord!

TRUTH:
Did we wake up this morning? Did we just inhale? We are to praise God for who He is and if we have breath, we are to use it to praise Him.

RESPONSE:
Lord, You've just allowed me to take another breath. Because I have breath, I will use it to praise You. I praise You!!

About the Author

Several years ago, God led Kristi Burchfiel through some difficult times in her personal life. Only by studying and applying the truths found in the Bible did she find the answers she needed to get her life back on track.

Now, Kristi works daily to continue putting those truths into practice. She is passionate about studying and applying the Bible and invites others to share in the peace and direction of God found through the truths in God's word.

Kristi, her husband D, and their two children currently make their home in Wichita, Kansas.

Website – www.kristiburchfiel.com
Twitter – http://twitter.com/#!/kristiburchfiel
Facebook -
http://www.facebook.com/#!/pages/Without-Regrets-A-Study-of-Ecclesiastes/122149427808582

Also by Kristi Burchfiel

Bible Studies:

The Decay Within: A Study of Amos

Amazon:
http://amzn.com/1618620142

Tate Publishing:
http://www.tatepublishing.com/bookstore/book.php?w=978-1-61862-014-9

Without Regrets: A Study of Ecclesiastes

Amazon:
http://amzn.com/1615665005

Tate Publishing:
http://www.tatepublishing.com/bookstore/book.php?w=978-1-61566-500-6

The Daily Devotional Series:
The Daily Devotional Series: Gospel of John
The Daily Devotional Series: Genesis
The Daily Devotional Series: Psalm volume 1
The Daily Devotional Series: Psalm volume 2
The Daily Devotional Series: Psalm volume 3
The Daily Devotional Series: 365 Devotions Through the New Testament
The Daily Devotional Series: 1 & 2 Chronicles
The Daily Devotional Series: Proverbs

How to Become a Christian

- We are all sinners
  - Romans 3:23 – *for all have sinned and fall short of the glory of God*
- The result of our sin is that we all deserve death
  - Romans 6:23 – *For the wages of sin is death, but the free gift of God is eternal life in Christ Jesus our Lord.*
- God paid the penalty for our sins on our behalf through the death of his Son, Jesus Christ
  - Romans 5:8 – *But God demonstrates His own love toward us, in that while we were yet sinners, Christ died for us.*
- When we acknowledge our sin and understand God's free gift of salvation, accept God's gift and allow Him to be Lord of our life, he saves us.
  - Romans 10:9-10, 13 – *that if you confess with your mouth Jesus as Lord, and believe in your heart that God raised Him from the dead, you will be saved; for with the heart a person believes, resulting in righteousness, and with the mouth he confesses, resulting in salvation. For whoever will call on the name of the Lord will be saved.*

Admit that you are a sinner, believe that God has provided a way through Jesus for you to be saved, and confess or pray to God and ask Him to be the Lord of your life. He loves you!

John 1:12 – *But as many as received Him, to them He gave the right to become the children of God, even to those who believe in His name.*

Made in the USA
San Bernardino, CA
16 January 2020